HE- Brews

Crystal M. Holm & Joshua L. Holm

S.T.E.P.

Cover Design by Crystal M. Holm
Visit the author's website at www.themanofsteel.com

Printed in the United States of America

ISBN: 978-0-9863737-4-9

CONTENTS

ACKNOWLEDGMENTS

I would like to thank God for inspiring me to write a devotional. The encouragement of who I am that I am able and good enough. My husband Joshua Holm for helping me with some of the context and questions. Our first devotional with hopefully many more to come.

The Cup

*Sustaining all things by His
powerful word.
Hebrews 1:3b NIV*

I don't know about you but I personally have a cup of coffee every morning before my day starts. Just like that coffee gets me going and wakes me up so should prayer and reading the word be. Hebrews starts even by saying in 1:3 sustaining ALL things by His powerful word.

Coffee changes the water just like the word changes you. The slower the drip the stronger the coffee. The more water you put in it the weaker it becomes. Coffee for most people helps them wake up (connect) ie coffee is like Christ the more of Him the bolder you are.

Daily Drip

God, I pray not to rush through my time with You as if checking off a list. Instead help me to brew in Your presence. Stir that desire in me for You like I long for that first cup. Let me be aware of Your presence and what You're saying throughout the day. Even if it's just a moment like the one I take to wrap my hands around the cup and enjoy those first few sips let me be intentional about enjoying You. Help me to become strong and bold just like coffee. Amen

Espresso

1. Take time to read all of Hebrews one.

2. How can you slow drip in God's presence?

3. What's in your cup if you're a cup for the King?

Oil of Joy

*You have loved righteousness and hated
wickedness;
therefore God, your God, has set you above your
companions
by anointing you with the oil of joy.*
Hebrews 1:9

I don't know about you but me I LOVE that first cup of coffee in the morning. I mean let me be honest I love coffee anytime. There's just something about wrapping your hands around a warm cup. Even more so than that coffee, Christ brings me lasting joy. Oil is needed in your car to keep the engine from locking up. Oil keeps things moving without causing friction. It's hard to explain but even in the hardest most difficult times we can still have joy. Things can be falling apart around you but if you focus on God and all the things, He's done for you instead of your problems you can have joy. It's just like that moment in the morning with your coffee. You wrap your hands around the cup take in the aroma and think about nothing else but enjoying that first sip.

Daily Drip

God thank You for Your joy that fills my cup. I thank You for Your anointing oil and Your care for me. Help me to rest in Your presence. Let my eyes stay focused on you. Your goodness surrounds me like that warm cup of coffee and there is no fragrance sweeter than You. Thank You for pouring Your oil over me.

Espresso

1. What is keeping you from having joy in your life?

(This is not to dwell on but identify it and remove it from stopping the flow.

2. What is causing friction? Where do you need more oil?

3. How can you take in the aroma of Christ more?

Pay Careful Attention

*We must pay the most careful attention, therefore,
to what we have heard, so that we do not drift
away.*
Hebrews 2:1 NIV

The filter is needed during the percolating process. It keeps the grounds out of your cup. Almost no one likes grounds in their coffee. The filter must be changed after every pot. Why do you think the word encourages us to be aware and awake because we can drift away? We can become distracted by the cares of this world. Even though I don't like it there are times a few grounds slip through and are floating around in my cup. Ugh, but if I'm paying attention, I can spot them before I consume them. Take every thought captive and filter it with God's word.

Daily Drip

Lord, I thank You that You have given us the word to filter life and things through. God, I pray You help me to consume more of Your word and Your presence so that I can pay careful attention to what's in my cup. Help me to remove all debris and grounds not of You. Thank You for continuing to help me grow. Amen

Espresso

1. What trash or debris has come through your filter that needs to be removed?

2. What is distracting you?

3. Does your filter need to be changed?

Mindful of Him

*We must pay the most careful attention, therefore,
to what we have heard, so that we do not drift
away.*
Hebrews 2:6-8 NIV

Let's think about the coffee bean for a minute. The coffee bean is a seed. Interesting as when the seeds are removed, they are dried and cleaned in preparation for roasting. We are supposed to be like seeds planted and fruitful. The coffee bean goes through a process before ever reaching your cup. Just like master roasters are mindful of the bean in the process so is our heavenly Father mindful of us. The master roasters look for smell, sip, slurp, and savor in coffee. God looks at every part of us as well. He has crowned us with honor and glory.

Daily Drip

God thank You for being mindful of us. I'm grateful You are even more concerned with the details of my life than master roasters are with coffee. Continue to help me know how much I mean to You. Your love and care know no end and I'm grateful for it.

Espresso

1. Just as the coffee is green and has to be cleaned. Are you clean?

2. What are you doing to savor the day?

3. How will you remind yourself that you matter to God?

Rest

*Therefore, holy brothers and sisters, who share in
the heavenly calling, fix your thoughts on Jesus,
whom we acknowledge as our apostle and
high priest.*
Hebrews 3:1 NIV

Fixing or preparing coffee takes work. Fixing your thoughts on Jesus takes work and time. If you think of the process from growing the bean to our cup it's work. Thankfully we can buy the coffee already ground and ready. We can even buy it in pods ready in moments not even waiting for the pot to brew. Fixing our thoughts on Jesus sometimes just requires us to rest and take time out of our schedule to intentionally spend time resting in Him.

Daily Drip

Lord thank You that You've given us Your word to know You more. Thank You for Your spirit that guides and comforts. Help me to fix my thoughts on You. Help me to meditate on Your word day and night. I thank You for purifying me.

Espresso

1. Think about fixing or preparing something it doesn't always come natural but it's worth it. How can you fix your thoughts on Jesus more?

2. What things do I need to work on?

3. Where can I make it a point to rest in my schedule?

Encourage Daily

*But encourage one another daily, as long as it is
called "Today," so that none of you may be
hardened by sin's deceitfulness.*
Hebrews 3:13 NIV

Every day I wake up and have a cup of coffee. If I have coffee daily, why wouldn't I encourage myself and others in the things of God. Just like that cup of joe every morning we need to encourage ourselves so that we can encourage others. Have you ever missed that morning cup? I have and boy could I tell. We need daily fuel physically, mentally, and spiritually.

Daily Drip

Thank You, Lord, that we can come to You anytime. Thank You that we are called to encourage one another. Daily we need Your fuel just like coffee. Help me to seek You more. Help me to hear Your voice more clearly. Help me to be bold in encouraging others. I thank You for the body of believers. I thank You that we are called to encourage one another.

Espresso

1. How can I encourage someone today?

2. What can I do to spend more time with God daily?

3. How can I be encouraged by others?

Rest Still Stands

*Therefore, since the promise of entering his rest still
stands, let us be careful that none of you be found
to have fallen short of it.*
Hebrews 4:1 NIV

Have you ever left coffee in the pot? Over time it becomes stronger and bolder the longer it rests. We need time to rest as well. Heaven is our eternal rest but we need to rest in God's presence here on Earth as well. There are times when we need short periods of rest and there are times, we need longer periods of rest. The percolating process takes moments of rest if you have ever watched the coffee pot it sucks up a little bit of water and then heats it and pours over the grounds, then it drips it into the pot.

23

Daily Drip

Lord thank You for giving us rest. Thank You for the promise of Heaven and eternal rest. Help me to trust You and to learn to   rest   in Your presence. Help me not to worry and to stand strong on Your word. Thank You for continuing to guide me and lead me when I need rest. Amen

Espresso

1. What is stopping me from resting?

2. How can I learn to rest?

3. How can I allow things to pour over me?

Nothing Hidden

*Nothing in all creation is hidden from God's
sight. Everything is uncovered and laid bare before
the eyes of him to whom we must
give account.*
Hebrews 4:13 NIV

Coffee beans are tested through, a sample roasting process to reveal their characteristics and uncover any hidden defects prior to production. Nothing is hidden from God; He sees us and all of our defects we go through testing so that our characteristics are brought to light to us. This is why we should rejoice in testing because it revels the hidden things in our hearts. God is constantly cultivating that which is good in us.

Daily Drip

Lord thank You for bringing to light any defects within myself. Help me to continue to come into Your presence of roasting so that I may be purified. Help me find joy in the process. I thank You for drawing me and loving me unconditionally because You see me as You created me not as I am currently.

Espresso

1. What has been brought to light that I can change?

2. How can I be more open to what God has for me?

3. Is there a time of testing that I can find joy in?

process

⁷ During the days of Jesus' life on earth, he offered up prayers and petitions with fervent cries and tears to the one who could save him from death, and he was heard because of his reverent submission. ⁸ Son though he was, he learned obedience from what he suffered
Hebrews 5:7-8 NIV

Harvesting coffee beans is a process. First the fruit is picked and then processed. After being dried they are milled this removes the skin and outer stuff. Then the beans are inspected and defective ones are discarded. The green coffee is now sent off to be tasted and this is all done before the final roasting process. Just as Jesus went through a process and learned obedience through what He suffered and made perfect; he became the source of eternal salvation for those who obey Him we go through a process. The process may not be easy but it is worth it. The reward just like that cup of coffee in the morning is worth it. The beans must be dried to 11% dry. What if the process was stopped early the coffee wouldn't be as good.

Daily Drip

Lord, I thank You for the process. I thank You for taking the time to help me. God help me to find joy in the process because the process isn't my purpose. Help me to not become impatient in the process. Thank You for equipping me in the process for my purpose just as You did Jesus.

Espresso

1. Read James 1:2-4

2. Write your joy in the journey below

3. Where am I in this season of process?

Constant

But solid food is for the mature, who by constant use have trained
themselves to distinguish good from evil
Hebrews 5:14 NIV

Knowing God and serving Him is constant. Just like the drying out of the coffee beans and the constant raking in order to prevent spoiling. We must be constantly learning to prevent spoiling or falling away. Eager to learn and understand. If we become stagnant and not moving or being raked like the beans, we can become bitter (or spoiled). Our relationship with God must be constant and tended too.

Daily Drip

God thank You for caring for us more than those who prepare coffee beans. Thank You for prodding us to seek You. Help me to hunger and thirst for Your righteousness. Help me to grow in You and no longer need elementary truths. God, I thank You for giving me what I need to grow and not become bitter.

Espresso

1. What area of your life needs to be exposed to the sun (SON) to prevent spoiling?

2. In what areas do I need to grow?

3. How can I help rake (stir) those around me to prevent spoiling?

Taste

[4] It is impossible for those who have once been enlightened, who have tasted the heavenly gift, who have shared in the Holy Spirit, [5] who have tasted the goodness of the word of God and the powers of the coming age [6] and who have fallen[a] away, to be brought back to repentance. To their loss they are crucifying the Son of God all over again and subjecting him to public disgrace. [7] Land that drinks in the rain often falling on it and that produces a crop useful to those for whom it is farmed receives the blessing of God. [8] But land that produces thorns and thistles is worthless and is in danger of being cursed. In the end it will be burned.
Hebrews 5:14 NIV

Once you've tasted a smooth quality cup of joe there is nothing else like it. It is the same way with God. You taste and see how good He is, nothing else satisfies like He does. Yeah, you might be able to drink the cheaper watered-down coffee but does it really satisfy like a smooth quality cup? When we don't put in what it cost for the quality and goodness of God thorns and thistles can begin to produce. Instead let's be like a well-watered and rick soil, a smooth quality coffee.

Daily Drip

Thank You, Lord, that I am watering my soil with You by doing devotionals and Bible studies. Help me to continue to taste and see that You are good. Help me to see if any thorns or thistles are trying to take root in my life. Thank You for Your goodness and the richness of your quality.

Espresso

1. What am I willing to do to share in the Holy Spirit?

2. Can you identify any thorns or thistles that are trying to take root in your life?

3. Take time throughout your day to sip on the goodness of God.

Patience

[12] We do not want you to become lazy, but to imitate those who through faith and patience inherit what has been promised.
[13] When God made his promise to Abraham, since there was no one greater for him to swear by, he swore by himself, [14] saying, "I will surely bless you and give you many descendants."[a] [15] And so after waiting patiently, Abraham received what was promised.

Hebrews 5:14 NIV

Patience, who likes to wait, no one. If we didn't wait for the coffee beans to go through the process, we would have coffee just not flavorful coffee. Roasting the beans brings in the aroma and flavor we all long for. Patience isn't easy but the reward is worth it. Just like Abraham received what was promised to him after he waited patiently, we can have faith knowing in the vault of patience is found victory.

Daily Drip

God thank You that You keep Your promises. Help me to stand firm in faith with patience even when I cannot see how or when the promise will be fulfilled. Help me to wait patiently gracefully. Thank You that You encourage me while I wait.

Espresso

1. Is there a promise that I'm waiting for now?

2. How can I wait patiently, in faith?

3. Is there a dream or promise you have given up on due to waiting?

Perfection and Order

¹¹ If perfection could have been attained through the Levitical priesthood—and indeed the law given to the people established that priesthood—why was there still need for another priest to come, one in the order of Melchizedek, not in the order of Aaron?
Hebrews 7:11 NIV

There is an order in the Kingdom of God just like an order to preparing coffee. If any order would work then it wouldn't be such a process to make coffee from seed to cup. Not any order will do though because the bean must be prepared. The roasting process is one that must not be skipped. God has an order and it's not for us to understand every step of His order but just to do the step He has us on.

Daily Drip

God, I thank You that Your thoughts are higher than my thoughts and that Your ways are higher than my ways. God help me to not try to change the order of things You would have me to do. Help me to trust the process even when I might not understand. Thank You for always having the perfect timing and showing me when I'm open to receive.

Espresso

1. How can I identify if I am in order or out of order?

2. In what simple ways can I help align myself in Gods order?

3. Reflecting on decisions was there peace, joy, and other fruits of the spirit? Decisions you've made that were in order?

New Identity

14 For it is clear that our Lord descended from Judah, and in regard to that tribe Moses said nothing about priests. **15** And what we have said is even more clear if another priest like Melchizedek appears, **16** one who has become a priest not on the basis of a regulation as to his ancestry but on the basis of the power of an indestructible life. **17** For it is declared: "You are a priest forever, in the order of Melchizedek."[a] **18** The former regulation is set aside because it was weak and useless **19** (for the law made nothing perfect), and a better hope is introduced, by which we draw near to God. **20** And it was not without an oath! Others became priests without any oath, **21** but he became a priest with an oath when God said to him: "The Lord has sworn and will not change his mind 'You are a priest forever.'"[b] **22** Because of this oath, Jesus has become the guarantor of a better covenant. **23** Now there have been many of those priests, since death prevented them from continuing in office; **24** but because Jesus lives forever, he has a permanent priesthood. **25** Therefore he is able to save completely[c] those who come to God through him, because he always lives to intercede for them.

Hebrews 7:14-25 NIV

There is a beautiful thing that happens when

coffee grounds and water goes through the process of percolating. Coffee grounds turn into brewed coffee, not coffee water or water coffee just coffee. The grounds gain a new identity. Something beautiful happens to us when we come to God through Jesus. We gain a new identity and have someone who is continually praying for us. He makes us bold and strong just as the process of coffee being brewed and the grounds and water now have a bold and strong flavor.

Daily Drip

Lord, I thank You that You're the High Priest and that You truly meet our needs. I thank You for interceding for me. Thank You for giving me a new identity in You. You make all things new. You call us by who we are becoming and not by who we are in this moment. You take us through a process that changes us and I thank You for it. Help me to comply to the process. Amen.

Espresso

1. Are you living according to the law or a better covenant?

2. Are you allowing God to drip over you?

3. What is your identity, how do you see yourself?

Exact Pattern

5 They serve at a sanctuary that is a copy and shadow of what is in heaven. This is why Moses was warned when he was about to build the tabernacle: "See to it that you make everything according to the pattern shown you on the mountain.
Hebrews 8:5 NIV

I think our life with Christ can be very much like that of roasting coffee. God give us an exact pattern to follow. He gives us the basics in how we should live and uphold our lives. Just as He has time and time again given instructions on how to do things in the Bible. Every coffee is different just as every individual is different. Each process is a little different every calling is different but there are fundamental things that remain the same. Coffee roasting has three steps, drying, browning, roasting. God gives us an exact pattern to follow we just need to read the plan and ask Him what He has specifically for us. Don't get caught up comparing your process to others. There are light roast and dark roast coffees they are still coffees that go through an exact pattern process just with slight differences. The main process still remains the same.

Daily Drip

Lord thank You for having an exact process and plan for my life. Help me to seek You for direction and not get distracted looking at others process. The pattern You have for me is unique for my flavor qualities. I pray that I'm a sweet fragrance to You as I continue to follow the pattern You have for my life.

Espresso

1. In what ways can I identify the pattern for my life?

2. How have I strayed from the things God has already shown me?

3. What things are distracting me from following the pattern for my life?

The Timing

*10 This is the covenant I will establish with the
people of Israel
after that time, declares the Lord.
I will put my laws in their minds
and write them on their hearts.
I will be their God,
and they will be my people.*
Hebrews 8:10 NIV

Waiting on His timing can be difficult. There may be things you know that God has shown you but here you are again waiting on His timing. Just like coffee has a roasting time so does the things in our life. Roasting coffee beans too quickly can result in burning. There are times when roasting the beans quickly are desired but other times not. I think we may get caught up in things we know the best time for things to transpire in our lives but God knows the perfect time.

Daily Drip

God, I thank You for our perfect timing. I thank You that You're still working on me in the process so that I'm able to hold the weight of what You want to give me. Help me to wait with patience and gratitude. Help me to be thankful in the process.

Espresso

1. Are there things you are waiting on right now?

2. How can you be thankful while waiting?

3. What can you do to be mindful of the time?

The Arrangement

⁶ When everything had been arranged like this, the priests entered regularly into the outer room to carry on their ministry.
Hebrews 9:6 NIV

Just like in the tabernacle where everything had to be arranged for the priest to carry out their ministry things must be arranged for us to carry out ours. A coffee shop wouldn't be very successful if they didn't have the equipment to grind, press, and brew the coffee. Certain things need to be arranged in our lives to carry out certain things God has called us to. The great news is that even while preparing and arranging things God is still moving and still using us. He doesn't let everything not being in order hinder us. No matter where you are in getting things arranged continue to move forward.

Daily Drip

Lord thank You for arranging my life. Help me to continue to move forward even with the work ahead. Help me not to become discouraged or overwhelmed. I pray that I find strength in the work and lean on You and not myself.

Espresso

1. Are there ways that I have complicated the task before me?

2. Where have I relied on my own strength and not God's?

3. In what ways can I arrange my life to prepare for what God has for me?

Untainted

> **13** The blood of goats and bulls and the ashes of a heifer sprinkled on those who are ceremonially unclean sanctify them so that they are outwardly clean. **14** How much more, then, will the blood of Christ, who through the eternal Spirit offered himself unblemished to God, cleanse our consciences from acts that lead to death,[a] so that we may serve the living God!
> *Hebrews 9:13-14 NIV*

Did you know that coffee can become tainted or fermented if the fruit is left too long on the bean? Also, microorganisms can enter the coffee and cause it to become tainted. These tainted beans are still cleaned and used but the residue of the fermentation can still sightly be tasted. This reminds me of our lives tinted by sin. Our flavor and aroma aren't pleasing when we are tainted. Great news through Christ blood cleanses us and causes us to be untainted. He cleanses us better than the ceremonial blood sprinkling. Christ comes and makes us new. It would be like the coffee bean gets to start fresh a clean slate.

Daily Drip

Lord thank You that Your cleansing is perfect. I thank You for the clean slate. God help me to live a life pleasing to You. I thank You that I can have a fresh start and a life untainted due to Your sacrifice.

Espresso

1. Have I accepted Christ sacrifice for my life?

2. Are there areas of my life where I've picked up old sin habits?

3. How can I remove the things that are hindering me?

Sacrifice

[10] They are only a matter of food and drink and various ceremonial washings—external regulations applying until the time of the new order.
Hebrews 10:10 NIV

For me in the morning I wake up and enjoy that first cup of joe. I sip it not even thinking of the sacrifice it takes to make it. My effort in making it was easy I press the brew button and viola there is my morning cup. There were many steps in getting that coffee in my hands. Individuals sacrificed their time they put in labor for me to enjoy my coffee. God sacrificed His only Son for me to enjoy salvation once and for all. Neither was an easy task both came with work, patience, and determination.

Daily Drip

God thank You for Your perfect sacrifice. Thank You for taking the time to provide a perfect example for us. You are God and could have sacrificed Christ immediately but instead allowed Christ to live as an example for us. Help me to be an example to my peers. Help me to not continue to deliberately keep sinning. Help me to always be mindful of the sacrifice You made.

Espresso

1. In what ways have I become complacent?

2. Are there ways I can be a better example?

3. Dig Deeper Read all of Hebrews 10

Draw Near

22 let us draw near to God with a sincere heart and with the full assurance that faith brings, having our hearts sprinkled to cleanse us from a guilty conscience and having our bodies washed with pure water.
Hebrews 10:22 NIV

Recently we planted fruit trees and I had no idea how much water they needed when first planted. The same is true for coffee beans. Coffee beans are planted during the wet season, so that the soil remains moist while the roots become firmly established. We are told to draw near to Christ so that our roots can become firmly established. Water is needed for growth and cleansing spiritually and physically. Christ is the living water so if plants need water to grow and survive how much more do we need to draw near to Him. Plants thrive when watered, how much more will we thrive when watered.

Daily Drip

God, I thank You that You are the living water. I thank You that we can draw near to You. Help me to firmly establish my roots in You. Help me to draw from our cup. Thank You for encouraging me and giving Yourself.

Espresso

1. How can I draw near to Christ?

2. What areas of my life am I neglecting to water?

3. Dig Deeper Read John 4:7-14

Faith

*⁸ By faith Abraham, when called to go to a place
he would later receive as his inheritance, obeyed
and went, even though he did not know where he
was going.*
Hebrews 11:8 NIV

Abraham the father of faith went in obedience to a place later to become his inheritance, even though he didn't know where he was going. The coffee farmers do not know what type of harvest they will have but plant in faith believing they will harvest a crop of coffee beans. We are supposed to live this way with faith, not knowing the outcome but having faith knowing who has our best interest in mind. Faith just as it states in Hebrews 11:1 KJV Now faith is the substance of things hoped for, the evidence of things not seen.

Daily Drip

God thank You for the examples of faith You have given us. Help me to have faith in all areas of my life. Help me to live with the confidence of knowing that You have my best interest in mind. Help me to step out boldly in faith. I thank You that our hope is found in You.

Espresso

1. What am I believing God for?

2. Are there areas I'm doubting?

3. In what ways can I strengthen my faith?

Seven Days

*30 By faith the walls of Jericho fell, after the army
had marched around them for seven days.*
Hebrews 11:30 NIV

Joshua and the children of Israel marched around the walls of Jericho for 7 days. They didn't murmur or complain while marching around the walls. How does this relate to coffee you might ask. Well for espresso roast profiles, it is suggested to rest your coffee for at least 7 days to degas. The children of Israel complained often but in order to win the battle they had to take a rest from murmuring or complaining. It's very beneficial for us to step back and rest from our daily routine. How might our lives be different if we challenged ourselves to end murmuring and complaining for just 7 days.

Daily Drip

God, I thank You that we can win our battles. I thank You that You give us a battle plan. God help me to rest from the routine of murmuring and complaining. Help me to change to an attitude of gratitude. I pray You continue to shine a light on the areas I need to change and I thank You for it.

Espresso

1. How often do I find myself complaining?

2. How could I change my perspective on areas I murmur or complain about?

3. Write things you are thankful for and read Philippians 2:14-16

No Pain No Gain

¹¹ No discipline seems pleasant at the time, but painful. Later on, however, it produces a harvest of righteousness and peace for those who have been trained by it.
Hebrews 12:11 NIV

In most countries, the coffee bean crop is picked by hand in a labor intensive and difficult process. Just as the coffee pickers have a painful enduring time it yields an amazing harvest. We get to enjoy the satisfying cup in the morning due to someone else's labor. Discipline in our Christian walk yields a harvest that is pleasant even though the process is painful. The coffee pickers who have been trained I'm sure have an easier time yielding a harvest as it is with as we are trained by discipline.

Daily Drip

God thank You for Your discipline. I thank You for training me and guiding me. God help me to see discipline as something good and not negative. God continue to guide me as I navigate this life. Thank You for loving me.

Espresso

1. Looking back how has God's discipline helped me?

2. What areas of my life need more discipline?

3. What areas can I have a little grace on myself?

Bitter Root

*15 See to it that no one falls short of the grace of
God and that no bitter root grows up to cause
trouble and defile many.*
Hebrews 12:15 NIV

It's funny that the scripture warns a bitter root growing and defiling many. Did you know that there is a parasite that can attack the roots of the coffee bean plant? They weaken the root system and cause the plant to not produce a harvest. This can be the case in our lives if we allow bitterness to take root. It not only affects us but those around us. One plant can become infested and effect the whole crop.

Daily Drip

God thank You for Your grace. Help me to identify bitter areas in my life. Help me to remove them and begin the healing process. God thank You for speaking to me and helping me to not be a victim. Thank You for helping me be victorious in every area of my life.

Espresso

1. What areas am I bitter?

2. How has my bitterness affected others?

3. What boundaries can I put in place to help prevent bitterness?

64

The Fruit aka the Seed

*15 Through Jesus, therefore, let us continually offer
to God a sacrifice of praise—the fruit of lips that
openly profess his name.*
Hebrews 13:15 NIV

The coffee bean is housed inside the fruit. During coffee production the fruit is typically discarded. This makes me think of the fruit of our lips. How easily we speak without even considering the seeds we are producing? How often do we utter words without thinking of the consequences? There is power of life or death and it is in the tongue. Reference (Proverbs 18:21) Fruit comes from a seed just as the coffee fruit comes from the coffee bean seed. The fruit is the product of the seed so let's plant good seeds with our words.

Daily Drip

God thank You for breathing life into me. Help me to breathe life with my words. Help my speech be pleasing to You. God help me to plant seeds of righteousness with my mouth. Let me not so easily discard what I'm saying as if it doesn't carry weight.

Espresso

1. What type of seeds am I producing with my words?

2. How can I change my speech?

3. Dig deeper read Philippians 4:8

Work

²¹ Equip you with everything good for doing his will, and may he work in us what is pleasing to him, through Jesus Christ, to whom be glory for ever and ever. Amen.
Hebrews 13:21 NIV

We drink our coffee in the morning and it begins its work in us. Coffee can make you feel refreshed and focus. It is a natural diuretic and helps boost energy levels. God does the same thing for us when we allow Him to work in us. We feel energized and focused and He flushes out the waste we do not need. There are days I need an afternoon pick me up with a cup of coffee and there are certainly days that I need to get an extra cup of Jesus.

Daily Drip

God thank You for working in me. Help me to allow You to work in me and equip me. Help me to trust You with every area of my life. There may be some days that I need to break from my routine and allow You more room to work and that is ok. Thank You for being available always.

Espresso

1. Are there areas in my life where I need to allow God to work more?

2. What areas have I grown in?

3. Dig Deeper read Colossians 3:23-24

Foundation

¹⁰ He also says, "In the beginning, Lord, you laid the
foundations of the earth,
and the heavens are the work of your hands.
Hebrews 1:10 NIV

Foundations are usually laid before anything else takes place. The Lord laid the foundations of the earth in the beginning. The land is prepared and has to be the correct conditions in order for the coffee plant to grow. Fun fact the seed is prepared as well. God knows the beginning and the end and He has already made the preparations. This is really encouraging and should help us to trust Him.

Daily Drip

God thank You for laying the foundation. God, I thank You that You are the beginning and the end. There is nothing that surprises You. Help me to trust You more. Help me to surrender every area of my life to You.

Espresso

1. In what areas do I need to trust more?

2. How am I encouraged by the passage in Hebrews 1?

3. What foundational work can I do?

Suffering

⁹ But we do see Jesus, who was made lower than the angels for a little while, now crowned with glory and honor because he suffered death, so that by the grace of God he might taste death for everyone. ¹⁰ In bringing many sons and daughters to glory, it was fitting that God, for whom and through whom everything exists, should make the pioneer of their salvation perfect through what he suffered.
Hebrews 2:9-10 NIV

Not sure if you have heard the story about the carrot, egg, and coffee bean but here is the shortened version. All three were put in boiling water, a period of suffering. The carrot turns soft, the egg hard, and the coffee bean changes the hot water. The coffee bean changed the water! Christ changes us, He endured the suffering of the cross to bring us salvation. Coffee goes through an intense process to bring us our favorite cup but nothing like what Christ endured to bring us salvation.

Daily Drip

God thank You for changing us. Thank You for suffering for my sake. Help me to remember Your sacrifice. Help me not to take Your suffering for granted. May my life be true reflection of You. I'm thankful for the purification process which requires suffering. Thank you Lord for helping me in my own suffering which is nothing compared to Yours.

Espresso

1. How can I change my perspective during suffering?

2. Are there times where I can look back and be thankful for suffering?

3. Rejoice in suffering! Dig Deeper read Romans 5:3-5

Bold

16 Let us therefore come boldly to the throne of grace, that we may obtain mercy and find grace to help in time of need.
Hebrews 4:16 NKJV

Bold coffee is usually right in your face and tastes strong with the first sip. There is a difference between strong and bold coffee. Strong coffee refers to the water to coffee ration when bold coffee is an intense full bodies rich flavored coffee. Bold coffee is strong and smooth in nature full bodies with no bitter taste. Just like bold coffee in your face we can approach the throne of grace with boldness. A confidence that we find in Christ knowing He already knows our flaws, our strengths, our everything. He wants a relationship with us one where we communicate. After one sip of bold coffee there is no doubt as to what you are drinking. We should approach Christ with no doubt of His love for us.

Daily Drip

God thank You that we can approach Your throne of grace with boldness and confidence. Thank You for loving me unconditionally. Help me to have a willing heart and to continue in confidence. Let it not be pride but confidence because of who You are. I thank You that You help me in my times of need.

Espresso

1. What hinders me from approaching God boldly?

2. What are the qualities of strength I see in myself?

3. How does Christ see me?

Pure

26 Such a high priest truly meets our need—one who is holy, blameless, pure, set apart from sinners, exalted above the heavens. 27 Unlike the other high priests, he does not need to offer sacrifices day after day, first for his own sins, and then for the sins of the people. He sacrificed for their sins once for all when he offered himself.
Hebrews 7:26-27 NIV

There is something about a pure cup of coffee. Coffee that is free from impurities and additives. Beans that have been grown without pesticides. The same is true for us as Christians we needed a sacrifice that was pure without spot or blemish. But Christ came and He was set apart. He was pure, holy, and blameless. Christ sacrificed Himself so that we wouldn't have need for the ceremonial sacrifices.

Daily Drip

God thank You for Your sacrifice. Thank You for being pure and holy. I owe a debt I cannot repay but help me Lord to be more like You. Help me to strive for holiness and purity. God continue to mold me and make me. God, I thank You for loving me and dying for me. May I think of You every time I drink a cup of coffee. May I fix my thoughts on You.

Espresso

1. Are there impurities in my life?

2. What do I desire spiritually?

3. Dig Deeper study holiness
   2 Corinthians 7:1, 1 Peter 1:15-16, Hebrews 12:14, Psalm 119:9, 1 Corinthians 3:16

Maturity

¹ Therefore let us move beyond the elementary teachings about Christ and be taken forward to maturity, not laying again the foundation of repentance from acts that lead to death,[a] and of faith in God, ² instruction about cleansing rites,[b] the laying on of hands, the resurrection of the dead, and eternal judgment. ³ And God permitting, we will do so.
Hebrews 6:1-3 NIV

Coffee plants can take three to five years before they produce any fruit. After they came to maturity is when the bean can be harvested. During spring after the harvest, the plants are pruned to yield even a greater harvest. We as Christians should be like the coffee bean plant and mature. After maturing we need pruning to yield more fruit. I think sometimes we resist the pruning process and/or growth. There is so much more to being a Christian than just repentance as there is more to coffee production than just the growing of the plant. Without the process we wouldn't have coffee. May we be diligent as Christians and want to grow and mature. You obviously are as you have chosen to do this devotional. May you have fruit that will multiply from generation to generation. I pray a blessing over you for maturity and growth.

Daily Drip

God thank You that You desire for us to grow and mature. Help me to seek You in all that I do. Help me to continue in growth and not become stagnant. May I allow You to prune me when needed. Help me to live a life that shines brightly for You, bringing glory to You!

Espresso

1. In what areas do I see maturity in my life?

2. What are some areas that I need to grow?

3. Be thankful in pruning. Read Hebrews 12:9-11

ABOUT THE AUTHORS

Crystal M. Holm is the CEO for Steel Hope. She has taken on management roles her whole life starting as the oldest sibling of two. Crystal has been a team leader, manager, president, and business owner. Her passion for helping others became very evident in high school with volunteering in National Honor Society. She is native Texan that grew up in Arkansas where she met her husband, Joshua, the father of their two beautiful children. In 2002, Joshua and Crystal moved to Killeen, Texas as a young military family. Her life would never be the same after Joshua's deployment to Iraq. Steel Hope was birthed out of her and her husband's testimony of hope and continued healing after all of Joshua's injuries from serving. Crystal is a published author of the children's book "The Adventures of Steel". She is a certified instructor with Military School for Ministry with Global University partnered with REAP International a division of the Roever Foundation. She is mental health first aid certified and has obtained certifications through the Military Veterans Peer Network as a Peer Support Specialist and Peer Group Facilitator. Her passion and compassion are unmistakable.

Crystal's motto: "Extraordinary lives are lived out in ordinary moments."

Joshua L. Holm, the Founder of Steel Hope, has always had a heart for others. His primary role as the Chief Visionary Officer at Steel Hope is to keep the vision intact. He has a love for all people, but a special place for people with mental and physical disabilities. Due to both physical and mental disabilities that were sustained while serving in the military, Joshua has a passion to help others with injuries. Joshua is a very passionate individual with a drive and enthusiasm that is undeniable.

He has a desire to restore our communities one person at a time. Joshua has begun by becoming a certified mentor through the Tarrant County Veterans Court (Vet Court). He has also obtained certifications through the Military Veterans Peer Network as a Peer Support Specialist and a Peer Group Facilitator. He is mental health first aid certified as well. Furthermore, he is a motivational speaker, life coach, and a published author.

For more information about Joshua L. Holm
visit www.themanofsteel.com

Joshua's philosophy in life: "Reflect on the past, perfect the present, to protect the future."

Joshua's motto: BE STEEL

www.ingramcontent.com/pod-product-compliance
Lightning Source LLC
LaVergne TN
LVHW051426080426
835508LV00022B/3265